ALADDIN
AND THE ENCHANTED LAMP

Aladdin is a lazy boy. He does not like work and he plays all day with his friends in the market. He and his mother are very poor, and are often hungry, but Aladdin never works, and never helps his mother.

One day Aladdin's uncle, Abanazar, arrives in the city. 'I am a rich man,' he tells Aladdin and his mother. He gives them gold, buys Aladdin a beautiful new coat, and wants to help them. Aladdin is very happy.

But Abanazar is not Aladdin's uncle. He is a magician from Morocco, and he wants to find an enchanted lamp. He knows the lamp is in a magical garden under the ground, near a city in Arabia. Only a poor boy from the city can get into the garden and find the lamp. And that boy's name is Aladdin . . .

OXFORD BOOKWORMS LIBRARY
Fantasy & Horror

Aladdin and the Enchanted Lamp

Stage 1 (400 headwords)

Series Editor: Jennifer Bassett
Founder Editor: Tricia Hedge
Activities Editors: Jennifer Bassett and Alison Baxter

RETOLD BY JUDITH DEAN

Aladdin
and the
Enchanted Lamp

Illustrated by
Thomas Sperling

OXFORD UNIVERSITY PRESS

OXFORD
UNIVERSITY PRESS

Great Clarendon Street, Oxford OX2 6DP

Oxford University Press is a department of the University of Oxford
It furthers the University's objective of excellence in research, scholarship,
and education by publishing worldwide in

Oxford New York

Auckland Bangkok Buenos Aires Cape Town Chennai
Dar es Salaam Delhi Hong Kong Istanbul Karachi Kolkata
Kuala Lumpur Madrid Melbourne Mexico City Mumbai Nairobi
São Paulo Shanghai Taipei Tokyo Toronto

ISBN 0 19 422937 8

Fifth impression 2003

First published in the Oxford Bookworms Library 2000

Printed in Spain by Unigraf s.l.

CONTENTS

1
Help from a rich man

Many years ago, in a city in Arabia, there was a boy called Aladdin. He lived with his mother in a little house near the market, and they were very poor. Aladdin's mother worked all day, and sometimes half the night, but Aladdin never helped her.

He was a lazy boy and he did not like to work. He only wanted to play all the time. Every morning he ran

Aladdin lived in a little house near the market.

through the streets to the market. There, he talked and laughed and played with his friends all day. Then in the evening he went home for his dinner.

And every night his mother said to him: 'Oh, Aladdin, Aladdin! You are a lazy boy – a good-for-nothing! When are you going to do some work, my son?'

But Aladdin never listened to his mother.

One day in the market there was an old man in a long black coat. Aladdin did not see him, but the old man watched Aladdin very carefully. After some minutes he went up to an orange-seller and asked:

'That boy in the green coat – who is he?'

'Aladdin, son of Mustafa,' was the answer.

The old man moved away. 'Yes,' he said quietly. 'Yes, that is the boy. The right name, and the right father.'

Then he called out to Aladdin: 'Boy! Come here for a minute. Is your name Aladdin? Aladdin, son of Mustafa?'

Aladdin left his friends and came to the old man. 'Yes,' he said, ' I am Aladdin, son of Mustafa. But my father is dead. He died five years ago.'

'Dead!' said the old man. 'Oh, no!' He put his face in his hands and began to cry.

'Why are you crying?' asked Aladdin. 'Did you know my father?'

The old man looked up. 'Mustafa was my brother!' he

The old man went up to an orange-seller.

said. 'I wanted to see him again, and now you tell me he is dead. Oh, this is not a happy day for me!' Then he put his hand on Aladdin's arm. 'But here is my brother's son, and I can see Mustafa in your face, my boy. Aladdin, I am your uncle, Abanazar.'

'My uncle?' said Aladdin. He was very surprised. 'Did my father have a brother? I didn't know that.'

'I went away before you were born, my boy,' said the

old man. 'Look.' He took ten pieces of gold out of his bag, and put them into Aladdin's hands. 'Go home to your mother and give this money to her. Tell her about me, and say this: "Her husband's brother wants to meet her, and he is going to visit her tomorrow."'

He put the ten pieces of gold into Aladdin's hands.

Ten pieces of gold is a lot of money and Aladdin was very happy. He ran home quickly and gave the gold to his mother. At first she was afraid.

'Where did you get this, Aladdin? Did you find it? It isn't our money. You must give it back.'

'But it *is* our money, Mother,' said Aladdin. 'My uncle, my father's brother, gave the money to us. Uncle Abanazar is coming to visit us tomorrow.'

'Who? You don't have an uncle Abanazar.'

'But he knows my name, and my father's name,'

Aladdin said. 'And he gave ten pieces of gold to me. He's very nice. You must make a good dinner for him.'

The next day Abanazar arrived at Aladdin's house.

'My sister!' he said and smiled. 'My dead brother's wife! I am happy to find you and Aladdin.'

'Sit down, Abanazar. We're happy to see you in our poor home,' Aladdin's mother said. She put meat, rice and fruit on the table. 'But I don't understand. Why did my husband never speak about you?'

'I'm sorry, my sister. When we were young, my brother and I were not friends for many years. Then I went away to a far country. I am an old man now and wanted to see my brother again and take his hand. But

Aladdin's mother put meat, rice and fruit on the table.

Abanazar had tears in his eyes.

he is dead, and I cannot speak to him or say goodbye to him now!'

Abanazar had tears in his eyes and Aladdin's mother began to cry too.

'But I am home again now,' the old man said, 'and I can help my brother's wife and his son, because I am a rich man.' He looked at Aladdin. 'Aladdin, my boy, what work do you do?'

Aladdin did not answer and his face was red.

'Oh, don't ask Aladdin questions about work!' his mother said. 'He never works. He plays with his friends all day, and only comes home when he is hungry.'

'Well, my boy, tomorrow we must get a new coat for you. Then we can talk about work. Would you like to have a shop in the market perhaps?'

Aladdin smiled. 'A shop,' he thought, 'and me, a rich market-seller. Why not?'

2
A walk to nowhere

Early the next morning, Abanazar arrived at Aladdin's house and then he and Aladdin walked to the market.

'First of all we must look at coats,' Abanazar said.

Soon Aladdin had an expensive new coat and he felt very happy. Then Abanazar and Aladdin walked through the market and looked at the shops. They drank coffee, talked to people, and had a very good dinner. It was a wonderful day for Aladdin.

On Friday, when the market was closed, Abanazar took Aladdin to the beautiful gardens in the city. They walked under the trees and talked about a shop for Aladdin.

Aladdin had an expensive new coat.

They walked past the Sultan's palace.

'You are very good to me, Uncle,' Aladdin said.

Abanazar smiled. 'But of course,' he said. 'You are my brother's son. Now, let us leave the city and go up into the hills. There is something wonderful there, and you must see it.'

They left the gardens, walked past the Sultan's palace, and out of the city up into the hills. They walked for a long time and Aladdin began to feel tired.

'It's not far now,' said Abanazar. 'We're going to see a beautiful garden – more beautiful than the garden of the Sultan's palace.'

At last Abanazar stopped. 'Here we are,' he said.

Aladdin looked, but he could see no gardens on the hills. 'Where is this garden, Uncle?' he said.

'First we must make a fire,' said Abanazar.

Aladdin did not understand, but he made a fire for his uncle on the ground. Then Abanazar took some powder out of a small box, and put it on the fire. He closed his eyes and said, '*Abracadabra!*'

At once, the sky went dark. Black smoke came from the fire, and the ground under the fire began to open.

Abanazar put some powder on the fire.

9

There was a big white stone with a ring in it.

Then the smoke went away, and in the ground there was now a big white stone with a ring in it.

Aladdin was very afraid. He began to run away, but Abanazar took his arm and hit him on the head.

For a minute or two Aladdin could not speak or move. Then he cried, 'Why did you do that, Uncle?'

'You must be a man now, not a child,' said Abanazar. 'I am your father's brother, and you must obey me. Don't be afraid. In a short time you're going to be a rich man. Now, listen carefully.' He took Aladdin's hand. 'Only you can move this stone. Put your hand on the ring and say your name and your father's name.'

Very afraid, Aladdin put his hand on the ring. It was not hot, but very cold. 'I am Aladdin, son of Mustafa,' he said. The stone moved easily, and now Aladdin could see stairs under the ground.

'Go down those stairs,' Abanazar said, 'and then through four big rooms. In the last room there is a door into a garden, and under one of the trees there is a lamp. You can take some fruit from the trees, but first you must find the lamp. Bring the lamp to me.'

'Please come with me, Uncle!' Aladdin said.

'No. Only you can do this, my boy.' Abanazar took a gold ring off his finger and gave it to Aladdin. 'This ring is magic and can protect you,' he said. 'Be careful, and bring me the lamp quickly!'

Aladdin put the ring on the little finger of his left hand

Aladdin put the ring on his finger.

11

and began to go down the stairs. It was dark and he was afraid, but he was more afraid of Abanazar.

And Aladdin was right to be afraid, because Abanazar was not his uncle. He was a magician from Morocco, and he wanted this lamp very much. It was a magic lamp, and only a poor boy from the city could get it for him – a boy called Aladdin.

Aladdin went down a hundred stairs and into the first room. Down here, it was not dark and he went quickly through the rooms to the door into the garden. There were trees in the garden, with beautiful fruit of different colours – white, red, green, and yellow.

He soon found the lamp, under one of the trees. 'Why does my uncle want this dirty old lamp?' he thought. He put it in his pocket. Then he began to take fruit from the trees, and to put it in every pocket of his coat. After that he went back to the stairs and began to go up. Soon he could see Abanazar and the blue sky.

'Give the lamp to me,' Abanazar said, and put out his hand. 'Quickly, boy, the lamp!'

Aladdin could not get the lamp out of his pocket because it was under the fruit. He looked at Abanazar's angry face and was afraid.

'First help me out, then you can have the lamp,' he said. 'Please, Uncle!'

'First the lamp,' cried Abanazar. 'Give me the lamp!'

Aladdin found the lamp under one of the trees.

'No!' Aladdin said.

'You good-for-nothing! You dog! You and the lamp can stay down there!' Angrily, Abanazar ran to the fire and put more powder on it. '*Abracadabra*!' he called.

The big white stone moved again, and now Aladdin could not see the sky. He was in the dark, under the ground, and could not get out.

3
The ring and the lamp

'Uncle Abanazar! Uncle!' Aladdin hit the stone but nothing moved. 'Don't leave me here! Please!'

Aladdin put his ear to the stone, but he could hear nothing. 'I am Aladdin, son of Mustafa,' he said, and listened again. But the stone did not move.

Then Aladdin began to cry. 'What am I going to do?' he thought, and put his head in his hands.

After a time he began to feel hungry, and took some of the fruit out of his pocket. He put some in his mouth, but he could not eat them. 'These are stones, not fruit,' he thought. 'I'm going to die down here.'

For three days and three nights Aladdin sat on the stairs and waited, but no help came. On the third day he remembered Abanazar's ring on his finger – the ring to protect him. He could not see the ring in the dark so he put his right hand on it . . .

WHOOSH!

There was a sudden noise, and blue smoke came out of the ring. And then, out of the smoke came a big jinnee.

'I am here, master, I am here,' the jinnee cried. 'I am the slave of the ring. What is your wish?'

Aladdin was very surprised, and very afraid. At first

Out of the smoke came a big jinnee.

he could not speak, then he said, 'Take me out of here.'

'To hear is to obey,' the jinnee said, and a second later Aladdin was back on the hills under the blue sky.

There was nobody there, and the fire was cold and black. Happily, Aladdin began to walk home.

When he got there, his mother was very happy to see him. 'Oh, Aladdin!' she cried. 'What happened to you? And where is your uncle?'

'Abanazar is not my uncle, Mother. He is a magician and a bad man. He nearly killed me.' Then Aladdin told his mother all about the fire, the magic stone, and the garden under the ground. 'Oh, I am very tired, Mother,' he said. 'I must sleep.'

Aladdin closed his eyes and slept for many hours. The next morning he opened his eyes and said: 'Mother, I'm hungry!'

'My son, I'm sorry,' she said. 'We have no rice or meat in the house. We have nothing. I must sell your new coat and get some rice with the money.'

Then Aladdin remembered the lamp from the garden.

'Wait a minute, Mother,' he said. 'Take this lamp and sell that first.'

'That dirty old thing?' Aladdin's mother said. 'I must clean it first.' She began to rub it and . . .

WHOOSH! Noise, fire, and red smoke came from the ͻ, and out of the smoke came a very big jinnee.

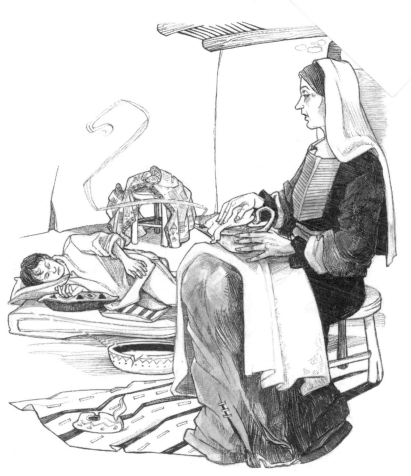

Aladdin's mother began to rub the old lamp ...

'I am the slave of the lamp,' cried the jinnee. 'What is your wish, mistress?'

Aladdin's mother was afraid and could not speak, but Aladdin said: 'Bring rice and meat to us. We are hungry.'

The jinnee went away, and came back in a secon

*The jinnee came back with rice, meat, bread and fruit
on twelve gold plates.*

with rice, meat, bread, and fruit on twelve gold plates.
He put the plates in front of them and went away.

Aladdin and his mother ate and ate. Then Aladdin
took one of the plates to the market and sold it for two
pieces of gold.

Every day after that, Aladdin rubbed the lamp. And
when the jinnee came, Aladdin said: 'Bring us rice and
meat.' And every day he sold the gold plates.

Soon, Aladdin and his mother were rich.

4
Aladdin's love

Five years later, Aladdin had a shop in the market and three market-sellers worked for him. The sellers liked Aladdin because he was good to them. The market children liked Aladdin too, because he gave them money when he walked past. Everybody liked Aladdin.

Aladdin's mother never called her son a good-for-nothing now. They had a nice house near the gardens and she had many beautiful things. But only Aladdin and his mother knew about the magic lamp and the jinnee.

The market children liked Aladdin too.

Six slaves carried the Princess in a litter.

One day Aladdin heard a noise in the street and stopped to listen. 'The Sultan's daughter is coming,' he heard. 'Princess Badr-al-Budur is coming!'

Six slaves carried the Princess through the streets in a litter, and the people stopped to watch. 'Princess! Princess Badr-al-Budur!' they called.

Aladdin watched when the litter came past him, and he saw the Princess's face. She was beautiful, with big dark eyes – the most beautiful woman in Arabia. The litter went past Aladdin, but for some minutes he did not move. Then he ran home.

'Mother! Mother! I saw the Sultan's daughter, Princess Badr-al-Budur, in the street.' Aladdin's face was white. 'I must have the Princess for my wife!'

'But, Aladdin . . .' his mother began.

'No "buts", Mother. I love the Princess and I want to marry her. Go to the Sultan and ask for me.'

'Me? Go to the Sultan's palace? No, no, no,' Aladdin's mother said. 'Listen, my son. The daughters of a Sultan do not marry poor boys from the city.'

'But we are not poor now, Mother. And we can give the Sultan something for his daughter. Wait.'

Aladdin went away and got the fruit from the magic garden under the ground. Now, of course, he knew it was not fruit, but white, red, green, and yellow jewels.

'Take these jewels, on a gold plate,' said Aladdin.

'Take these jewels, Mother, on a gold plate,' he said, 'and give them to the Sultan.'

So the next day Aladdin's mother carried a gold plate with many beautiful jewels on it to the Sultan's palace. She went into a long room, but when she saw the Sultan, his Vizier, and all his slaves, she was very afraid. So she waited quietly in the room and spoke to nobody. In the evening she went back home again with the jewels. Aladdin was very angry with her.

'Mother, you must speak to the Sultan,' he said. 'I have no father to do this for me. You must help me – I must marry the Princess. I love her!'

So the next day, and for many days after that, Aladdin's mother went to the palace, but she was always afraid to speak.

In the end, the Sultan saw her and asked his Vizier: 'Who is that woman? Why does she come to the palace every day?'

The Vizier spoke to Aladdin's mother: 'Do you want to speak to the Sultan? Yes? Come with me.'

The Vizier took Aladdin's mother to the Sultan, and she put her head on the ground at his feet.

'Get up, woman. Why do you come here every day?' the Sultan asked. 'Speak, woman.'

'Your Majesty,' Aladdin's mother said quietly, 'I have a son, a good young man. He is called Aladdin. He loves your daughter, Princess Badr-al-Budur. He cannot sleep or eat because of her. He wants to marry her.'

The Sultan laughed. 'What? Marry my daughter? Your son?'

'Your Majesty, these jewels are for you, from my son Aladdin.' And Aladdin's mother put the gold plate with the jewels in front of the Sultan's feet.

Aladdin's mother put the gold plate in front of the Sultan's feet.

Everybody looked at the jewels, and the long room was suddenly very quiet. Then the Sultan spoke.

'These are very beautiful jewels,' he said. 'No man in Arabia has jewels more wonderful than these. Your son is a rich man – a good husband for my daughter.'

The Vizier did not like to hear this, because he wanted the Princess to marry *his* son.

'Your Majesty,' he said quietly in the Sultan's ear, 'my son is a rich man, too. Give him three months, and he can find better jewels than these.'

'Very well,' said the Sultan. And to Aladdin's mother he said: 'Your son must wait for three months, and then perhaps he can marry my daughter.'

Aladdin's mother went home to tell Aladdin, and the Vizier went away to speak to his son. And every day, for two months, the Vizier's son came to the Sultan and gave him gold, and jewels, and many beautiful things.

For two months Aladdin waited happily, but one day his mother came home from the market and said:

'Oh, Aladdin! Aladdin! The Princess is going to marry the Vizier's son! I heard it in the market. Everybody's talking about it.'

When Aladdin heard this, he was very unhappy. 'What can I do?' he thought. He put his head in his hands and thought for a long time. And when night came, he took out the magic lamp and rubbed it . . .

The jinnee came back with the Princess asleep in his arms.

WHOOSH! 'What is your wish, master?' said the
jinnee of the lamp.

'Bring Princess Badr-al-Budur to me,' said Aladdin.

'To hear is to obey.'

In a second the jinnee was back with the Princess
asleep in his arms. He put her carefully on a bed, and
then the Princess opened her eyes and saw Aladdin.

'Who are you?' she asked, afraid.

Aladdin took her hand and looked into her eyes. 'My
name is Aladdin, and I love you,' he answered. 'I cannot
live without you, and I want to marry you.'

Badr-al-Budur saw the love in his eyes, and smiled.

She closed her eyes again, then the jinnee carried her back to the Sultan's palace. The next morning she remembered Aladdin's eyes. 'There is no love in the eyes of the Vizier's son,' she thought. 'He thinks only of gold and of jewels.' So the Princess went to her father.

'I do not want to marry the Vizier's son,' she said. 'I want Aladdin for my husband.'

The Sultan was very surprised. 'What can we do?' he said to his Vizier. 'My daughter wants to marry this man Aladdin. He is a rich man, it is true – but who is he?'

'Ask him,' said the Vizier quickly, 'for more of those beautiful jewels, on forty gold plates. And forty slave-girls, with forty slaves. Nobody is *that* rich.'

'Very good,' smiled the Sultan, and said to his slaves: 'Bring Aladdin's mother to me.'

When Aladdin's mother arrived, the Sultan said: 'So! Your son wants to marry my daughter. But first he must give me forty gold plates with jewels. Forty slave-girls, with forty slaves, must carry the plates to me. Then my daughter can be his wife.'

Aladdin's mother went home and told her son, and Aladdin smiled. This was easy for the jinnee of the lamp, of course, and the next day, when Aladdin went to the palace, everybody in the city came out to watch.

First came forty slave-girls in dresses of gold, and every girl carried a gold plate with wonderful jewels on

Everybody in the city came out to watch.

it. After them walked forty slaves in coats of gold. And last came Aladdin, on a beautiful white horse.

'What do you say now?' the Sultan said quietly to the Vizier, when he saw all these wonderful things. 'Aladdin *must* marry my daughter. How can I say no?' And the Sultan went to Aladdin and took his hands. 'My son,' he said. 'You can marry my daughter tonight.'

'Tomorrow, Your Majesty,' said Aladdin. 'Because, before I marry your daughter, she must have a palace – the most beautiful palace in Arabia.'

The jinnee of the lamp worked all night, and the next morning the Sultan saw from his window a beautiful new palace, with gardens of fruit trees and flowers.

'Wonderful!' he said.

'Black magic!' said the Vizier quietly.

That night Aladdin married Badr-al-Budur and they lived happily in the new palace.

'Black magic!' said the Vizier quietly.

5

New lamps for old

Where was Abanazar all this time? When he could not get the lamp from Aladdin, he went home to Morocco. He was very angry with Aladdin. 'But the boy is dead now,' he thought. 'And perhaps next year I can go back and get the lamp.'

One day, he got out his seven black stones. These stones were magic, and when he put them in water, the water could tell him many things. Soon, he could see the magic lamp in the water, but it was not under the white stone in the Arabian hills. It was in a palace.

'How did this happen?' said Abanazar. 'I must go back to Arabia and find this palace.'

Abanazar got out his seven black stones.

One day Aladdin and his friends went hunting in the hills.

After some months he arrived again in the city in Arabia. Soon, he saw the new palace and asked a man in the street: 'Who lives there?'

'That's Aladdin's palace,' was the answer. 'Princess Badr-al-Budur's husband, a good man – and very rich!'

Abanazar said nothing and walked away. 'That lazy, good-for-nothing boy!' he thought angrily. 'So he has the magic lamp, and he knows about the jinnee! How can I get the lamp back?'

For the next week Abanazar watched Aladdin's palace. One day Aladdin and his friends left the palace to go hunting in the hills.

'Good,' Abanazar thought, 'now I can get the lamp.'

After Aladdin left, Princess Badr-al-Budur went into the palace gardens. She sat under a tree and looked at the flowers. Then she heard a noise in the street, and called her slave-girl, Fawzia.

'What's the matter? Who's making that noise?' she asked. 'Fawzia, go and look in the street.'

When Fawzia came back, she had a smile on her face.

'Mistress,' she said, 'the children in the street are laughing at an old man. He's selling lamps, but not for money. "New lamps for old," he cries. "Give me an old lamp, and you can have a new lamp." So everybody's getting new lamps.'

Badr-al-Budur laughed. 'Do we have an old lamp for

31

him? Yes – my husband's old lamp! Go and get it.' The Princess knew nothing about the lamp or its magic.

Fawzia went into the palace and came back with Aladdin's lamp. 'Here it is, mistress,' she said.

'Go and give it to the old man.' The Princess laughed. 'Aladdin can have a nice new lamp!'

Fawzia went out into the street with the lamp. 'New lamps for old,' the old man called, and the children behind him laughed and called, 'New lamps for old.'

The old man (it was Abanazar, of course) saw the

'Aladdin can have a nice new lamp,' laughed the Princess.

'New lamps for old,' called the old man.

lamp in Fawzia's hands, and knew it at once, because of
the picture in the water of his magic stones. He took the
old lamp, gave a new lamp to Fawzia, and then quickly
walked away. He walked out of the city into the hills.
Then he took out the lamp and rubbed it . . .

WHOOSH! At once the jinnee of the lamp came to
him. 'I am here, master,' he said. 'What is your wish?'

'Carry Aladdin's palace, the Princess, and me back to
Morocco at once,' Abanazar said. 'The Sultan can kill
Aladdin for me.'

'To hear is to obey.'

In a second Abanazar, the palace, the gardens, and the
Princess were in Morocco. And in front of the Sultan's
palace there was now only a little red smoke.

6
There and back again

In the evening Aladdin and his friends finished hunting and began to go home. Suddenly a friend said: 'Aladdin, look! The Sultan's men are coming, with swords in their hands. What do they want?'

'I don't know,' Aladdin answered.

When the Sultan's men arrived, they said: 'Aladdin, we must take you to the Sultan. He's very angry.'

'Why?' asked Aladdin, but the men could not tell him.

'The Sultan's men are coming, with swords in their hands.'

In his palace the Sultan took Aladdin to a window. 'Where is your palace?' he cried angrily. 'And where is my daughter? Answer me!'

Aladdin looked out of the window. There was only the ground and the sky – no palace, no gardens, nothing. He closed his eyes, opened them and looked again, and he had no answer for the Sultan.

'It's black magic. I always said that,' the Vizier said quietly in the Sultan's ear.

'Your Majesty.' Aladdin put his head at the Sultan's feet. 'Kill me now – I do not want to live without Badr-al-Budur.' There were tears in his eyes.

'Find her in forty days – or you die,' the Sultan said.

'I hear and obey, Your Majesty,' Aladdin answered.

But without his magic lamp, what could Aladdin do? He went out from the city, and looked and looked for his wife and his palace, but of course he did not find them. After thirty-seven days he sat by a river and cried: 'Oh, Badr-al-Budur, my love! Where are you? Where can I look now?' He put his hands into the water of the river, and then he saw the magician's ring on his little finger. He began to rub it . . .

WHOOSH! Out of the blue smoke came the jinnee of the ring. 'What is your wish, master?' he asked.

'Find my wife and bring her back to me,' answered Aladdin. 'Please . . .'

'Master, I cannot do that. The jinnee of the lamp took the Princess away, and only the jinnee of the lamp can bring her back. But I can take you to her.'

'Take me then – quickly!'

'To hear is to obey.'

It is many, many miles from Arabia to Morocco, but Aladdin was there in a second. And there was his palace, in front of him. He went into the gardens and looked up at the windows.

'Badr-al-Budur,' Aladdin cried, 'are you there?'

'Badr-al-Budur,' he cried, 'are you there?'

In the palace Badr-al-Budur heard him. 'Is that Aladdin?' she thought. 'But he is far away in Arabia.' She went to the window, opened it, and looked out.

'Aladdin!' she cried. 'Oh, my love!'

For the first time in many days, Aladdin smiled.

'Come up, quickly!' the Princess called. 'The magician is not here now.'

Her slave-girl ran down and opened a little door into the gardens. Aladdin ran up to the Princess's rooms, and in a second she was in his arms.

'Oh, my love,' the Princess said. 'A bad man carried me here. A magician. His name is—'

'His name is Abanazar and I am going to kill him,' said Aladdin. 'Tell me – does he have my old lamp?'

'Yes,' Badr-al-Budur said. 'He always carries it with him. I know about its magic now, because he told me. Oh, why did I give it away?'

'Listen, my love,' said Aladdin. 'I'm going to give you some sleeping-powder. When he comes here again, you must give him a drink and put the powder in it. When he is asleep, I can kill him. Don't be afraid. I'm going to take you home very soon. Now for some good magic.'

He began to rub his ring . . .

WHOOSH! 'What is your wish, master?' said the jinnee of the ring.

'Bring me some sleeping-powder,' said Aladdin.

'To hear is to obey.'

In a second the jinnee was back with some sleeping-powder. Then Aladdin and the Princess waited for Abanazar.

In the evening they heard him on the stairs.

'Don't be afraid,' Aladdin said quietly to his wife. 'I am in the next room and can be with you in a second.' He went quickly into the next room and stood behind the door.

Abanazar opened the door of Badr-al-Budur's room and came in. He smiled: 'You are more beautiful every day, Badr-al-Budur,' he said. 'Your husband, that good-for-nothing Aladdin, is dead now. You must marry me. You can have gold, jewels, palaces, anything! But you must be my wife.'

For the first time the Princess smiled at Abanazar.

'Why not?' she said. 'You are a rich man and I am happy here. Yes, let's drink to that.'

And she gave him a tall gold cup with the drink and the powder in it.

'Let us drink from one cup, Abanazar,' she said, and smiled at him. 'You first, then me. In my country new husbands and wives always do this.'

'To Badr-al-Budur, the most beautiful woman in Morocco,' Abanazar said happily, 'and my wife.'

'Let us drink from one cup, Abanazar,' said Badr-al-Budur.

He looked into Badr-al-Budur's eyes and began to
drink. Very afraid, the Princess watched him. But it
was a good sleeping-powder, and after five seconds
Abanazar's eyes closed and he was asleep.

The Princess ran to the door of the next room.

'Quick, Aladdin,' she called.

Aladdin ran in with his sword and saw the sleeping
magician. 'Well done, my love!' he said. 'Now, go into
the next room and do not watch.'

Badr-al-Budur ran to the next room and closed the

'I am here, master,' said the jinnee of the lamp.

door. Aladdin put his hand in Abanazar's pocket and
took out the lamp. He put it carefully into the pocket of
his coat, and then stood up.

The sword did its work quickly, and Abanazar never
opened his eyes again.

The Princess came back into the room, and ran to
Aladdin. He took her in his arms.

'The magician is dead,' he said. 'And now we can go home.' He began to rub the lamp . . .

WHOOSH! Fire and red smoke came from the lamp. The Princess watched, afraid.

'I am here, master,' said the jinnee of the lamp. 'What is your wish?'

'Carry this palace, Badr-al-Budur, and me back to our city in Arabia. But leave that dog, Abanazar, here.'

'To hear is to obey,' said the jinnee.

*　*　*

When the Sultan looked out of his window and saw Aladdin's palace again, he was a happy man. And when he took his daughter in his arms, he was the happiest man in Arabia.

From that day, Aladdin and Badr-al-Budur lived happily in their palace. They lived for many years, and had many children. But Aladdin always carried the magic lamp with him, day and night.

GLOSSARY

abracadabra a magic word

jinnee a supernatural, magic spirit in Arabic stories

lazy a lazy person does not want to work

magic when strange, exciting, unusual things happen

magician a man in stories who can do magic

marry to take somebody as your husband or wife

master a man who gives orders to servants and slaves

mistress a woman who gives orders to servants and slaves

obey to do what somebody tells you

poor with very little money; not rich

protect to keep somebody (or something) safe

slave a worker who belongs to another person and who must work for that person for no money

sleeping-powder something which makes you sleep

Sultan a king; the most important man in an eastern country

surprised when something new, strange, or sudden happens, you are surprised

uncle the brother of your mother or father

unhappy not happy

Vizier an important man in an eastern country

wish something you want

Your Majesty when you speak to a Sultan, a King, or a Queen, you say 'Your Majesty'

Aladdin
and the Enchanted Lamp

ACTIVITIES

Before Reading

1 Read the back cover and the story introduction on the first page of the book. How much do you know now about the story? Tick one box for each sentence.

	YES	NO
1 Aladdin works all day in the market.	☐	☐
2 Abanazar comes to the city to find Aladdin.	☐	☐
3 Abanazar is Aladdin's uncle.	☐	☐
4 Aladdin can get into the magical garden, but Abanazar can't.	☐	☐
5 Abanazar wants to find gold and jewels.	☐	☐
6 There is a magical jinnee in the old lamp.	☐	☐
7 Aladdin is poor all his life.	☐	☐

2 What happens in this story? Can you guess? Choose words to complete these sentences.

1 Aladdin *finds* / *doesn't find* the lamp in the garden.

2 Aladdin *gives* / *doesn't give* the lamp to Abanazar.

3 Aladdin *marries* / *doesn't marry* the Princess.

4 Abanazar takes *the Princess* / *Aladdin* to Morocco.

5 Abanazar wants to *kill* / *marry* the Princess.

6 In the end *the jinnee* / *Aladdin* kills Abanazar.

7 The story has *an unhappy* / *a happy* ending.

While Reading

Read Chapter 1, and then answer these questions.

1 Why did Aladdin's mother call Aladdin a 'good-for-nothing'?
2 Where did Abanazar find Aladdin?
3 Why did Abanazar cry?
4 Why was Aladdin surprised?
5 What did Abanazar give to Aladdin?
6 Why was Aladdin very happy about this?
7 Who did Abanazar want to help?

Read Chapter 2. Choose the best question-word for these questions, and then answer them.

What / Where

1 . . . did Abanazar buy for Aladdin in the market?
2 . . . did Aladdin and Abanazar go after the city gardens?
3 . . . did Abanazar put on the fire?
4 . . . could Aladdin see in the ground under the fire?
5 . . . did Abanazar want Aladdin to go?
6 . . . did Aladdin put Abanazar's ring?
7 . . . was the lamp?
8 . . . did Aladdin put in every pocket of his coat?
9 . . . did Abanazar leave Aladdin and the lamp?

Before you read Chapter 3, can you guess what happens? Choose endings for these sentences.

1 Aladdin stays under the ground for . . .
   a) three hours   b) three days   c) three weeks
2 Aladdin sees his first jinnee. It comes out of . . .
   a) the old lamp   b) the white stone   c) Abanazar's ring

Read Chapter 3. Complete these sentences with words from the chapter (one word for each gap).

1 The jinnee of the _____ said, 'To hear is to _____.'
2 The second jinnee said, 'I am the _____ of the _____.'
3 Every day Aladdin _____ the lamp, and the jinnee came.
4 Aladdin _____ the gold _____ in the market.
5 Soon, Aladdin and his mother were _____.

Read Chapter 4. Who said this, and to whom?

1 'I must have the Princess for my wife!'
2 'He cannot eat or sleep because of her.'
3 'These are very beautiful jewels.'
4 'My son is a rich man, too.'
5 'The Princess is going to marry the Vizier's son!'
6 'Bring Princess Badr-al-Budur to me.'
7 'I do not want to marry the Vizier's son.'
8 'But first he must give me forty gold plates with jewels.'
9 'Black magic!'

Before you read Chapter 5, can you guess what happens next? Tick one box for each sentence.

	YES	NO
1 The Vizier finds the magic lamp and takes it.	☐	☐
2 Abanazar comes back to Arabia.	☐	☐
3 The Princess gives the lamp to Abanazar.	☐	☐
4 Abanazar takes Aladdin to Morocco.	☐	☐

Read Chapters 5 and 6. Then join these halves of sentences.

1 When Abanazar saw the lamp in the magic water, . . .
2 One day he walked in the streets by the palace . . .
3 Badr-al-Budur did not know about the jinnee . . .
4 Abanazar rubbed the lamp . . .
5 The Sultan was very angry with Aladdin . . .
6 The jinnee of the ring carried Aladdin to Morocco . . .
7 When Abanazar came to see the Princess, . . .
8 Then Aladdin came in and killed Abanazar . . .

9 but he gave him forty days to find the Princess.
10 and he and the Princess went home to Arabia.
11 he went back to the city in Arabia.
12 and the jinnee took him and the Princess to Morocco.
13 she put some sleeping-powder in his drink.
14 and called out, 'New lamps for old. New lamps for old.'
15 so she gave Aladdin's old lamp to Abanazar.
16 and he found his wife and his palace there.

After Reading

1 There are 21 words from the story hidden in this word search. Can you find them? The words go from left to right, and from top to bottom.

N	L	A	M	P	Z	U	R	J	G	F	I	R	E
B	S	O	A	C	I	T	Y	I	O	R	Q	S	P
P	T	M	G	A	R	D	E	N	L	U	W	U	O
O	A	H	I	L	L	S	V	N	D	I	I	L	C
W	I	X	C	G	T	I	R	E	D	T	S	T	K
D	R	E	I	S	T	O	N	E	M	C	H	A	E
E	S	O	A	Q	H	J	E	W	E	L	G	N	T
R	U	A	N	G	R	Y	E	R	U	B	B	E	D
P	A	L	A	C	E	O	V	I	Z	I	E	R	F

2 What did Aladdin tell his mother when he got home from the hills? Complete the passage with 15 of the words from the word search above. (One word for each gap.)

'In the _____ there is a beautiful _____ under the ground. Abanazar knew about it because he is a _____, and he wanted me to find a _____ under one of the trees. I found it and put it in my _____, with some _____ from the trees. But when I came back up the _____, Abanazar was _____ with me, so I didn't give him the lamp. Then he put more

_____ on the _____, and the magic white _____ moved again and I could not get out. In the end I remembered Abanazar's _____ ring. When I _____ it, a big _____ came out and put me back on the hill. Then I walked home. Oh, Mother, I'm so _____ – I must sleep now.'

3 **What did the Vizier say to his son when he went home? Put their conversation in the right order, and write in the speakers' names. The Vizier speaks first (number 3).**

1 _____ 'Yes, he does, but he's looking for a rich husband for his daughter. And Aladdin is very, very rich.'

2 _____ 'And what must I do in these three months?'

3 _____ 'My son, do you know a man called Aladdin?'

4 _____ 'But he can't! *I'm* going to marry Badr-al-Budur! And the Sultan knows that.'

5 _____ 'Go to the Sultan every day, my son. And give him gold, and jewels, and many beautiful things.'

6 _____ 'Then we must find some better jewels, Father.'

7 _____ 'I don't know, but he loves the Princess and he wants to marry her.'

8 _____ 'Is he? How do you know that, Father?'

9 _____ 'Yes, we must. The Sultan is giving us three months before he says yes to Aladdin.'

10 _____ 'No, I don't. Who is he?'

11 _____ 'Because today his mother gave the Sultan some beautiful jewels. The Sultan liked them very much.'

4 Here is a new illustration for the story. Find the best place
in the story to put the picture, and answer these questions.

The picture goes on page _____.

1 Who are the three men in the picture?
2 What can they see out of the window?
3 Where is Princess Badr-al-Budur at this moment?

Now write a caption for the illustration.

Caption: _____

5 Here is Aladdin's mother, talking about her son, but she says some untrue things. Can you correct them?

'No, I never called Aladdin a good-for-nothing when he was young! He was always a hard-working boy, and he liked to work. He never wanted to play. Now he has five shops, and twenty market-sellers work for him. We live in a palace, and soon Aladdin is going to marry the Vizier's daughter!'

6 There are a lot of magic things in this story. What did they do? Use this list to complete the sentences below.

the jinnee of the lamp   the seven magic black stones
the jinnee of the ring   the magic word 'Abracadabra'
the magic trees

1 _____ brought food every day on gold plates.
2 Abanazar said _____, and the ground opened.
3 _____ built Aladdin a beautiful palace.
4 _____ took Aladdin to Morocco.
5 When Abanazar put _____ in water, the water told him many things from far away.
6 _____ took the Princess to Morocco.
7 There were jewels, not fruit, on _____ in the garden under the ground.
8 _____ brought Aladdin some sleeping-powder.
9 _____ carried the Princess to Aladdin one night.

Which of these magic things would *you* like? Why?

ABOUT THE AUTHOR
AND THE STORY

Judith Dean was a teacher in Norway, Germany, and France for nineteen years, and now lives in Essex, in the east of England. When her daughter, Leah, was young, Judith Dean often told her stories about magic, like the story of Aladdin.

Aladdin and the Enchanted Lamp comes from a famous book called *Tales from the Arabian Nights*, or *The Thousand and One Nights*. The stories in this book are more than a thousand years old. They come from the Middle East and India, and first came to Europe three hundred years ago. Other famous stories in the book are *Ali Baba* and *Sindbad the Sailor*.

The stories in *The Arabian Nights* are all told by Shahrazad (or Scheherazade). She married a king, but he did not like wives and he always killed them after one night. Shahrazad did not want to die, so she told the King wonderful stories every night. When the sun came up, she stopped the story at an exciting place. The King always wanted Shahrazad to finish the story, so he did not kill her. And after a thousand and one nights, he liked his stories – and his wife – very much, and so he and Shahrazad lived happily for many years.

You can find the story of Aladdin in many places – in books, in the theatre, and in films. There is a famous Disney film of Aladdin, but that is a very different story from the one in this book.

ABOUT BOOKWORMS

OXFORD BOOKWORMS LIBRARY
Classics • True Stories • Fantasy & Horror • Human Interest
Crime & Mystery • Thriller & Adventure

The OXFORD BOOKWORMS LIBRARY offers a wide range of original and adapted stories, both classic and modern, which take learners from elementary to advanced level through six carefully graded language stages:

Stage 1 (400 headwords)	Stage 4 (1400 headwords)
Stage 2 (700 headwords)	Stage 5 (1800 headwords)
Stage 3 (1000 headwords)	Stage 6 (2500 headwords)

More than fifty titles are also available on cassette, and there are many titles at Stages 1 to 4 which are specially recommended for younger learners. In addition to the introductions and activities in each Bookworm, resource material includes photocopiable test worksheets and Teacher's Handbooks, which contain advice on running a class library and using cassettes, and the answers for the activities in the books.

————————————————

Several other series are linked to the OXFORD BOOKWORMS LIBRARY. They range from highly illustrated readers for young learners, to playscripts, non-fiction readers, and unsimplified texts for advanced learners.

Oxford Bookworms Starters	*Oxford Bookworms Factfiles*
Oxford Bookworms Playscripts	*Oxford Bookworms Collection*

Details of these series and a full list of all titles in the OXFORD BOOKWORMS LIBRARY can be found in the *Oxford English* catalogues. A selection of titles from the OXFORD BOOKWORMS LIBRARY can be found on the next pages.

The Wizard of Oz

L. FRANK BAUM

Retold by Rosemary Border

Dorothy lives in Kansas, USA, but one day a cyclone blows her and her house to a strange country called Oz. There, Dorothy makes friends with the Scarecrow, the Tin Man, and the Cowardly Lion.

But she wants to go home to Kansas. Only one person can help her, and that is the country's famous Wizard. So Dorothy and her friends take the yellow brick road to the Emerald City, to find the Wizard of Oz . . .

A Little Princess

FRANCES HODGSON BURNETT

Retold by Jennifer Bassett

Sara Crewe is a very rich little girl. She first comes to England when she is seven, and her father takes her to Miss Minchin's school in London. Then he goes back to his work in India. Sara is very sad at first, but she soon makes friends at school.

But on her eleventh birthday, something terrible happens, and now Sara has no family, no home, and not a penny in the world . . .

Pocahontas
RETOLD BY TIM VICARY

A beautiful young Indian girl, and a brave Englishman. Black eyes, and blue eyes. A friendly smile, a laugh, a look of love . . . But this is North America in 1607, and love is not easy. The girl is the daughter of King Powhatan, and the Englishman is a white man. And the Indians of Virginia do not want the white men in their beautiful country.

This is the famous story of Pocahontas, and her love for the Englishman John Smith.

The Adventures of Tom Sawyer
MARK TWAIN
Retold by Nick Bullard

Tom Sawyer does not like school. He does not like work, and he never wants to get out of bed in the morning. But he likes swimming and fishing, and having adventures with his friends. And he has a lot of adventures. One night, he and his friend Huck Finn go to the graveyard to look for ghosts.

They don't see any ghosts that night. They see something worse than a ghost – much, much worse . . .

The Phantom of the Opera

JENNIFER BASSETT

It is 1880, in the Opera House in Paris. Everybody is talking about the Phantom of the Opera, the ghost that lives somewhere under the Opera House. The Phantom is a man in black clothes. He is a body without a head, he is a head without a body. He has a yellow face, he has no nose, he has black holes for eyes. Everybody is afraid of the Phantom – the singers, the dancers, the directors, the stage workers . . .

But who has actually seen him?

Five Children and It

EDITH NESBIT

Retold by Diane Mowat

When the children dug a hole in the gravel-pit, they were very surprised at what they found. 'It' was a Psammead, a sand-fairy, thousands of years old.

It was a strange little thing – fat and furry, and with eyes on long stalks. It was often very cross and unfriendly, but it could give wishes – one wish a day. 'How wonderful!' the children said.

But wishes are difficult things. They can get you into trouble . . .